OXFORD

UNIVERSITY PRESS

ISBN 978-0-19-386014-8

www.oup.com

CELLO

JOHN RUTTER
WHAT SWEETER MUSIC

MUSIC DEPARTMENT

OXFORD
UNIVERSITY PRESS

CELLO

What sweeter music

for choir S.A.T.B. and string orchestra

JOHN RUTTER

Printed in U.S.A.